# Who Was Honda?

## A boy who pursued his dream

Mechanic

Engineer

Inventor

Author

Artist

By O. Snow

*enjoy!*

*O. Snow*

# Soichiro Honda
# The Founder of the Honda Corporation

Biography

(1905—1991)

© O. Snow
2018

## Also by O. Snow

*A Dog Lover* (YA fiction)

O. Snow—Who Was Honda?

# Contents

## Who Was Soichiro Honda?

When Soichiro Honda was four, engines fascinated him. His first dream was to drive cars. Then, when he was in elementary school, he wanted to be a car mechanic. He began by manufacturing piston rings, then bike motors, and finally he became the world leader in automotive production—the Honda Corporation.

Soichiro was born in 1906, in Shizuoka, Japan. Since his parents were poor, he wore the same dirty kimono day after day and seldom got a new one. The family that lived next door was wealthy. In the Boys' Festival in May, they decorated samurai dolls that Soichiro wanted to see. When he visited them, they said, "You're dirty. Don't come into my house!"

*Why did they discriminate against those who were poor?*

This memory was strong and stuck in his heart. When he stated his own business, his policy was that "everyone is equal."

He believed that if the company did not treat employees fairly, the company would not be successful. Soichiro wanted to be treated fairly, so he treated his employees in the same way. He was willing to spend money for pleasant working conditions; he paid for air conditioning and clean, beautiful restrooms. Soichiro regarded the work uniform as a technician's formal clothes, so he paid for cleaning his employees' uniforms. He provided warm, nutritious cafeteria food. His employees worked one of two shifts—from early morning to 3 p.m. or from 3 p.m. to midnight. He did not let them work after midnight because he viewed working late as detrimental to their health.

He said, "Having a clean environment is important in order not to damage the product."

When Soichiro hired someone, he always offered a full-time position. If his employees worked cheerfully and efficiently, he knew the company would benefit financially.

His parents taught him good life principles: "Don't lie, be punctual, keep your promises and don't cause trouble for others."

When he disobeyed one of those rules, he was spanked. So he tried to be on time, to keep any promise he made, and to always tell the truth.

Soichiro's goal was to make his business a company that did not cause trouble to people. When his company bought a large lot, he did not put a fence around it. He built beautiful bright buildings to make the residents happy. He also installed many lights around the building for safety and to give a good impression to the residents.

Soichiro was very sensitive to the problem of pollution. There were no laws about pollution when he began his business, so he developed his own standard. His company developed and managed to control the smoke and waste that came from his factory. All of his employees were proud of that.

Once in a while, there was a small mistake that disturbed the residents. Any complaint, no matter how small, were carefully addressed.

As his company grew to employ thousands, many employees never met him. But Soichiro loved and cared for them. He wished to shake hands with each one.

His dream came true when he retired. He and his wife Sachi traveled to seven hundred places in Japan over one-and-a half years. Then for six months, he visited his foreign installments. This was the first time he had met most of the workers. Soichiro said, "Thank you," and shook hands with each one. Tears dripped from his eyes. All of them were very impressed to meet Soichiro Honda, and many young employees cried.

"I was so happy when I visited them," he said. "I retired as company president, and then I met real people."

Soichiro pursued his dream all his life. He used his talents well and worked hard to achieve success. He greatly enjoyed what he accomplished and was willing to endure difficulties to reach his goals. And so he made his childhood dream come true.

# Chapter 1

## Engines

When Soichiro was four years old, he saw an engine for the first time. A rice polishing factory was near his house. *Boom, Boom.* The engine operated with a noisy sound. Once in a while, the factory's owner fixed the engine. Soichiro wanted to touch it, to see what it looked like and how it worked. This was the first time he showed an interest in mechanical things.

When he was eight years old, Soichiro saw an automobile passing by, blowing pale smoke from its exhaust as if it were a devil. Soichiro chased the car on his bicycle. He smelled the gas and touched it. He smiled.

O. Snow—Who Was Honda?

After that, Soichiro dreamed about touching an automobile. He wanted to drive one very fast. He believed that someday his dream would come true.

In 1917, when Soichiro was eleven years old, he heard that an airplane would fly in Hamamatsu City as part of an infantry corps display.

"I want to see the airplane!" He smiled.

On the day of the event, Soichiro got up early before anyone noticed, packed two sens, and rode his father's bicycle thirteen miles to Hamamatsu City.

When he arrived, he encountered a tall fence around the infantry corps area. It cost ten sens to enter, but he had only two. He was very disappointed, but soon Soichiro found a pine tree by the fence. He climbed up the tree, and he saw the airplane. It was only a glider with a simple motor, but he was very happy to see an airplane for the first time.

When he returned home, in his excitement the thirteen miles seemed like a much shorter distance. But in front of the house, his father stood waiting and he was angry.

However, when he found out Soichiro went to see the airplane, his father was impressed by his child's interest.

After that, Soichiro wanted to have a cloth hat like the one the pilot wore. He begged his father to buy him one. Then Soichiro wanted to have a pair of eyeglasses like the pilot had. But they were impossible to get in his small village. Since he was a handy boy, he made eyeglasses out of thick paper and walked around as if he were a pilot. He also made a propeller out of bamboo and placed it in front of the bicycle as if he were flying in the sky!

# Eugene Cernan

## (1934--)

Soichiro developed a strong interest in airplanes after he saw the air show. Later, he read about UFOs ("Unidentified Flying Objects"). When he visited NASA, he met astronaut Eugene Cernan. Cernan flew the Grumman F-14 Tomcat, the A-4 Skyhawk and other jets for the navy, then became an astronaut.

He went into space three times and walked on the moon twice. Cernan is the last man to walk on the moon. Soichiro wanted very much to ask him about life in space.

When Cernan visited Japan with his family, Soichiro invited them to his home. They enjoyed fishing for ayu, a sweet fish in the river behind his house.

Soichiro and Eugene became close, like father and son. They corresponded for over twenty years.

# Chapter 2

## Mischief

"I have no interest in a child who is not mischievous," Soichiro once said. Mischief is a motivating power to create something new. A mischievous child is full of originality and ingenuity. He must be allowed to enjoy discoveries and express himself.

Seeking the unknown is the same as the psychology that motivates an explorer. People tend to say "bad boy!" every time a child is mischievous. Soichiro thought that was the wrong attitude. The "bad boy" has a strong personality and the capacity to grow. He is really "a good boy."

When Soichiro was a child he poked holes the size of his hands in the watermelons in the garden and ate as much as he wanted. After finishing, he turned the watermelons over so the holes were hidden. His father punished him severely, but he enjoyed the watermelons!

When Soichiro went to the elementary school, there was a temple nearby with a garden full of persimmon trees. He often stole the fruit and enjoyed eating it. The monks did not approve.

When he was in third grade, he looked at the goldfish in the teacher's room. *They are all red: that's no fun*, he thought. He sneaked into the room and took each goldfish from the bowl and painted them with blue or yellow enamel. Then he put them back into the water. He thought they were beautiful. The principal found out and was furious, but Soichiro took joy in his mischief.

Because he did not like to study, he often sneaked away to a mountain behind the school. After playing there, he was hungry. Then he saw the temple bell and had an idea. The bell always rang at noon to announce lunchtime. Soichiro went to the bell and rang it, even though it was still 11 a.m. Then he went home and ate lunch. Of course his parents found out and punished him.

His next-door neighbor made stone *jizo* (one of the Japanese gods) statues. As Soichiro was artistic, he did not like the looks of the *jizo. If only I could fix his nose,* jizo's *face would look better,* he thought. One day, after his father went to work, Soichiro took a hammer and approached the *jizo*. The stone was hard and difficult to shape.

Suddenly, the whole nose fell off!

Soichiro was shocked and ran away. Many people said, "Terrible! The boy who did that kind of mischief must be Soichiro!"

Soichiro did not like any of his school subjects except science. When he was in fifth grade, he removed a magnet. The teacher attempted an experiment in front of his students. It didn't work, and he wondered why! After the teacher left the room, Soichiro put the magnet back and performed the experiment successfully. The students applauded.

After that, each time a mischief occurred, everyone said, "Soichiro did it again!"

In elementary school the teacher gave the students grades on their records. Grades ranged from A.B, C, and D to E. E was a failing grade. Soichiro did not receive an E, but he did get many Ds. He had to take the report card home for his parents to sign. His parents, instead of signing their names in ink, used a name stamp for the report card before returning it to the teacher.

Soichiro did not want to show his bad grades to his parents, so as a handy boy, he made a duplicate name stamp from the rubber of an old tire. He stamped the grade report himself and gave it to the teacher. Then other students wanted him to make stamps for them! He made several, but their parents found out. "Honda" is an easy *kanji* (Japanese character) to make, but some names had complicated *kanji* that were harder.

## Kanji, Hiragana, Katakana

*Kanji* came from China. Originally, *kanji* was comprised of pictographs; then in 10 B.C., the Chinese developed the pictures into over 8,000 letters. An average adult Japanese speaker must know at least 2,000 *kanji* by heart. Japanese children learn *kanji* from an early age every day, and they have to take *kanji* tests regularly in school. The Chinese, the Japanese and the Koreans still use *kanji.*

After using *kanji* for a while, the Japanese invented *hiragana* around 900 A.D.

*Hiragana* has forty-six letters in its alphabet. Today the Japanese use both *kanji* and *hiragana.*

Around 1300 A.D., the Japanese completed *katakana,* using some parts from *kanji,* which is also comprised of forty-six letters. *Katakana* uses the same pronunciation as *hiragana.*

The Japanese use *katakana* for foreigner's names, such as Mary, John or Mr. Smith, and for western products and sounds such as "television", "woof" or "meow".

# Chapter 3

## Dream, Hope, Persistence

When Soichiro approached graduation from Koto elementary school, he was absorbed in *Ringyo no Sekai* ("The World of Automobiles") magazine. Then he noticed a bulletin announcing that "Art Shokai" was looking for an apprentice.

*"Oh, yes. I will be an apprentice and learn about automobiles!"* Soichiro thought.

After he graduated from the Koto elementary school at the age of fifteen, Soichiro and his father rode the train from Hamamatsu city to Tokyo. Soichiro was full of hope. But being an apprentice was far from his dream. He couldn't even touch a car. His job was babysitting for his master's children instead of using a hammer or a wrench. He was even handed a cloth to clean the floor.

Soichiro was disappointed. To make matters worse, the other workers teased him because his kimono was always wet. He had to carry his master's baby around on his back. Every time the baby peed, his kimono got soaked, and the wet spot was just like a map.

"Your back has maps like China," the workers teased.

Soichiro had patience, but since he wasn't accomplishing his dream, he thought of going home many times. Still he stayed at Art Shokai because he had promised to become a repairman. If he came home, his parents would scold him for being spineless. So he thought as long as he could see these automobiles and look at the assembly and the machine structure, he was lucky.

Six months passed.

One cold, snowy day, his master called and said, "Boy! We are very busy today. You must help us. You can wear a uniform."

*Finally! I can use my best clothes,* he thought. He picked the uniform and wore it. Then he stood before a mirror. The uniform was old and dirty with oil, but he was happy indeed. It was big for him, but he looked at himself proudly.

"Hurry! You must come    right now," his master shouted.

Soichiro ran. Then his master pushed Soichiro into position under a car that was dripping water after its drive   through the snow. He had to remove the ice underneath. That was an easy job, but he enjoyed it. Anyway, he was working on a car!

"Oh, Boy! You do good work!" his master said after he inspected Soichiro's repair.

After that, his master let him repair cars instead of babysitting.

On September 1, 1923, at almost lunch time, the ground rumbled and buildings cracked! The Great Kanto Earthquake! It was difficult to walk straight or even stand.

Soon a fire from the earthquake reached Art Shokai. To prevent the customer's vehicles from burning, the company president said, "You must move the cars to a safer place!"

Soichiro was jubilant to drive the car he had just fixed. He had never driven before, but he didn't want to miss the opportunity. He jumped into the car and drove it to a safer place, avoiding the crowds of people. He was excited about driving the car and forgot all about the earthquake. This was the chance he had been waiting for!

After the earthquake, Art Shokai was burned, so they moved near the Kanda train station. After the disaster, Soichiro had to become a full-time repairman, because his boss had many burned cars to fix, and most of the repairmen had gone back home. With only two repairmen left, they had their hands full.

People were willing to buy the cars as long as the motor ran. The shop was able to sell at a high profit. At that time, all wheel spokes were made of wood, so they had burned in the fires and needed to be replaced. The shop craftsmen were proud of their ability to manufacture those wooden spokes on their own equipment.

O. Snow—Who Was Honda?

When Soichiro was sixteen, his master said, "Go to Morioka city to fix the fire department's fire engine. You can do it."

Soichiro was happy to see the scenery from the train window.

When he arrived in Morioka city after a ten-hour train journey, officials said, "Oh, a boy."

They were disappointed. Soichiro's cheeks burned red, but he did not speak, for he was only sixteen. The staff at the hotel where he stayed treated him like a child and placed him in a simple room next to the maids' quarters.

The next day, Soichiro took the engine apart.

Someone teased him: "Boy-san, you took so many things apart. Will you be able to put them back together?"

Soichiro clenched his teeth and tried not to show his embarrassment. Soon he finished the repairs, put all the parts back together, and fixed the engine perfectly.

"Oh! It runs, and the water hose works too!"

It seemed like a miracle to them. When he came back to the hotel, the manager invited him to the best room, and he was even served a delicious dinner with sake to drink.

Soichiro had matured from a little boy to an excellent repairman.

When he arrived in Tokyo, his master was very pleased to hear of the successful repairs. At the end of the month, Soichiro got five yen, his first salary.

Soichiro worked there for six years. He learned the skills of mechanical repair and how cars were constructed. Moreover, he could drive well. The first part of his dream had been realized.

# The Great Kanto Earthquake

## (Saturday, September 1. 1923)

The earthquake had a magnitude of 7.9, which meant it was very strong and destructive. The earthquake struck at lunchtime when people were cooking, so fire broke out all over the city. Many people died when their feet became stuck on the melting tarmac. The earthquake broke water mains and putting out the fire took nearly two full days. Almost 6,400 people were killed, and 381,000 houses were destroyed by the fire alone.

After the earthquake, Shinpei Gotho organized a reconstruction plan for Tokyo, with modern networks of roads, trains and public services.

Gotho was born in 1857, in Morioka, Japan. At first, he became a physician. Later he was involved in government. As he was very intelligent and knew how to solve problems, he had many important jobs.

# Ikuzo Sakakibara

## (1893--1974)

Soichiro started his own company at a young age. His employer was Ikuzo Sakakibara, the only boss Soichiro ever had.

Sakakibara was interested in auto racing, so he established an auto repair shop called Art Shokai. At that time, most cars in Japan were Model T Fords. Art Shokai repaired those cars, too.

At first, Soichiro worked as a babysitter, but soon Sakakibara discovered Soichiro's excellent talents. He taught Soichiro his skills, including how to treat customers and even how to start a new business. Moreover, he invited Soichiro to participate in auto racing. Soichiro joined the team as an engine mechanic. For the rest of his life, Soichiro was enthusiastic about racing.

Sakakibara allowed Soichiro to open a new branch of Art Shokai in Hamamatsu, his home town. Soichiro was the only person given this honor.

Soichiro was grateful to Sakakibara all of his life.

# Chapter 4

## <u>The Edison in Hamamatsu</u>

By 1928, Soichiro had learned everything about how to repair cars. He returned to Hamamatsu and established his own automotive repair shop. At first, this branch of Art Shokai was a simple, shabby facility with only one employee. And because Soichiro was so young, not many customers came for repairs. But soon they learned that he was very proficient in car repair. By the end of the year, he had a net profit of eighty yen. At that time, there were only a few automotive repair shops in town, so with little competition, Soichiro grew wealthy.

Soichiro was mechanically gifted: he even built an engine for a boat. It was successful, and he enjoyed riding in it with his employees.

In a few years, the number of his employees grew to fifty. Soichiro could find exactly which part of an engine had problems. His Hamamatsu repair shop grew famous, and the mechanics had the reputation of being able to fix any kind of car and to make repairs that other auto shops could not. He could even make a fire engine from a truck! In 1931, Soichiro invented iron spokes to replace the wooden spokes on tires and he invented many other things.

When he became wealthy enough to support his own family in 1933, Soichiro married

Sachi Isobe, a beautiful, highly educated woman. This was an arranged marriage.

In 1931, Soichiro had received one hundred fifty patents, and the Imperial Household gave him a prize. At the ceremony, His Highness Prince Takamatsu noticed that Soichiro was the youngest man there and talked to him.

"Invention must be hard, although I do not know too much about it," His Highness said.

Soichiro responded, "It is hard, but it is also fun."

Because of his inventions, many people called Soichiro "The Edison in Hamamatsu."

# Chapter 5

## The Worst Student?

Even though Soichiro invented many things, he was not satisfied. *If I take care of cars, I want to make an engine myself! Or at least I can make a part of the engine; something no Japanese has done yet …*

He decided to design a piston ring to protect the cylinders as the gas is burned in them. Soon, he stayed long hours at the factory and tried hard to make a good piston ring. He spent a lot of money, and soon his savings were gone. He even sold his wife's jewelry.

O. Snow—Who Was Honda?

Under great pressure, Soichiro visited Hamamatsu Koto Kogyo school—now called Shizuoka University.

"Umm … In Japan, no one has made a good piston ring yet. You are ambitious!" Fujii sensei (teacher) said. "I will ask one of our professors about it as soon as possible."

Soichiro bowed deeply in thanks.

A few days later, Tashiro sensei, who was a casting professional, told Soichiro, "The ring you developed needs more silicon, and the metal ratio is not right."

Soichiro did not even know what silicon was. When Tashiro sensei found out, it shocked him.

Now Soichiro realized the power of education. He decided to become a student. Soichiro was twenty-nine and drove a Nissan to school every day. To make a piston ring, Soichiro became serious.

But the school was not happy about Soichiro's attitude. Soichiro attended only the classes he really needed for his job, and he didn't even take the exam.

Soichiro, a president with fifty employees, wanted to take classes that only related to his work. He didn't care about the diploma. He neither failed nor was promoted, since he did not take all the required courses. His only purpose was making a good piston ring. The school had never had such a student before. He attended for two years. Usually, when a student attended three years, he could graduate from the school. The school expelled Soichiro, but he continued to attend classes and take notes. When he came home, he worked at his factory until 1 or 2 a.m.

Nine months later, on November 20, 1937, his hard work finally bore fruit: he made a piston ring successfully.

"The education   benefitted me," Soichiro said. "I learned the theory of technology, and I made the piston ring. The education was also useful in my later life. When I heard or saw something new, I could accurately judge it through the knowledge I gained at school, and it enabled me to produce something new. If we want to rise higher, we need a good basic education."

In 1939, Soichiro sold the Art Shokai Hamamatsu branch to one of his employees, and Soichiro established Tokai Seiki. He sold piston rings.

In 1994, the president of Yamaha asked Soichiro to make a machine that would produce wooden propellers. At that time, they made only one a week by hand, but Soichiro made a machine that could make two propellers every thirty minutes. The Japanese army praised Soichiro's excellent work.

Soichiro sold piston rings until the end of the war—they were for cars, ships and airplanes. After the war, few people needed ships or airplanes, so the piston ring business decreased.

In January 1945, the Mikawa earthquake destroyed Tokai Saiki factory.

After World War II, Soichiro stopped working for one year; he turned his attention to playing musical instruments and shogi, a Japanese game like chess. He also searched for a business that would be successful in the future.

# Eiji Toyota

## (1913—2013)

Toyota was Honda's rival company. But these two companies shared a good relationship. Eiji Toyota, the fifth president of Toyota, respected Soichiro as an excellent technician. Soon they became good friends.

Sakichi Toyota, the first president of Toyota, was Eiji's uncle. After Eiji graduated from Tokyo University, he started helping his cousin, Kichiro.

When Soichiro brought his piston rings to Toyota, Eiji examined them and met Soichiro for the first time. Soichiro amazed Eiji. "Soichiro is a real technician!" Eiji said.

O. Snow—Who Was Honda?

In 1967, Eiji became president of Toyota, and he transformed Toyota into a world business by using good manufacturing and sales methods.

In 1989, Soichiro Honda became a member of the Automobile Hall of Fame. In 1994, Eiji Toyota was the second Japanese person to receive this honor.

# Chapter 6

## Joy to Make, Joy to Sell, Joy to Buy

After World War II, Soichiro noticed the shortage of reliable transportation in Japan. He manufactured small engines and placed them on bicycles. One model was the *Type D Dream.* He sold many bikes, and he was a good mechanic, but he was not good in financial matters. His company was earning profits, but he did not know where the money went. He needed help. Then Takeo Fujisawa, who was not good at mechanics but was an astute financial manager, came to Soichiro.

At the end of their conversation, Fujisawa said, "From now on, you concentrate on mechanics, and I will take care of the money."

Soichiro agreed to everything Fujisawa proposed.

After 1949, when Fujisawa joined Soichiro, Honda Giken experienced great change. Soichiro "made" and Fujisawa "sold." Soichiro at forty-two and Fujisawa at thirty-eight made a competent team with the potential to lead the top company in Japan—and even in the world.

Fujisawa always insisted, "If we want to make inroads into foreign markets, we must take care of our brand. This must be the first priority."

Once an American trading company asked to buy a few thousand Honda products and sell them under the American company's name. Soichiro wanted to accept this offer. He didn't have much money, and it was an enticing proposal, but Soichiro sent Kawashima to America, where they found new markets on their own.

"Our patience and effort successfully established the Honda brand in foreign markets. We must uphold the honor of our own brand," Soichiro said.

In 1951, Honda released the motorbike model *Honda Dream Type E.* Its success made Honda a well-known company all over Japan.

In 1958, Honda produced the *Super Cub* model that women with skirts could drive. Woman did not like to get their skirts dirty, so Soichiro covered the oily chains and put the engine under the feet of the riders. Many women and even older people enjoyed riding the *Super*

*Cub.* It had a quiet four-stroke, single-cylinder engine that required little gasoline.

A few years later, Honda exported the *Super Cub* to America. Soichiro noticed that Americans used bikes for fishing and hunting, so he tried to sell the motorbike in sporting goods stores. The *Super Cub* could easily negotiate narrow mountain roads. He also advertised in *Time* and *Life* magazines, something that no motorbike company had done before. Honda's products sold well in America. From 1958 to 2008, more than sixty million were purchased. The *Super Cub* became the most popular motor vehicle in history.

## President Lyndon B. Johnson

(1908-1973)

When Honda began selling motorbikes in America, automobiles were the preferred method of transportation. Only a few people bought motorbikes. Many experts thought America would be a difficult market to break into. But Soichiro said, "If I could be successful in America—the best economy in the world—I could conquer the rest of the world!" With his great ambition, he was able to reach his goal.

When Honda first sold in America, the 36th president was Lyndon B. Johnson, who took office after John F. Kennedy was assassinated. Johnson served from 1963 to 1969. During his tenure, the Honda Super Cub became as popular in America as in Japan. Women and older people enjoyed riding on motorbikes. President Johnson said, "The Super Cub has changed the American lifestyle!"

# Chapter 7

## The Isle of Man T.T. Race

The Beautiful Isle of Man in Scotland hosts a very dangerous race each year. It is like an Olympic event for people who ride motorbikes. Many people from different countries dream about winning it. It is called the Isle of Man T.T. (Tourist Trophy) Race. Since 1924, England, France, Germany and Italy have poured their hearts into this international competition. Such a races led to the development of new and better engines, fuel injection devices, suspension systems and tires.

## O. Snow—Who Was Honda?

To win this historic race, a racing team must develop the best engine. Only the highest level of mechanical ability can secure a victory. A championship means the motorbike engine is the best in the world at the time, bringing prestige to the country that racing team represents.

Soichiro wanted to participate in the race. He welcomed the challenge. In 1954 he told his employees about his dream. Everyone was impressed. Soichiro visited the Isle of Man and studied the race and the motorbikes. He saw many excellent machines from England, Germany and Italy. He brought back many tools and mechanical parts from these motorbikes. The engines of the competition had thirteen horsepower, while Honda's had only nine. That was not powerful enough to participate in the race. The content standard was higher than Soichiro imagined. But he didn't give up. "We will win the race in a way no one has tried before." he said. "We must develop a whole new engine!"

For five years, the Honda team studied how to win the race. They spent a lot of money on research.

In 1959, a staff of nine mechanics went to the Isle of Man to compete.

When they checked in, people teased the Honda team. "Where are you coming from? Which country's motorbike are you going to use?" Obviously Honda was still not well known.

On June 3, 1959, at 1 p.m., the Tourist Trophy Race started. The Honda team ran persistently while many other motorbikes were unable to finish. The Honda team took $6^{th}$, $7^{th}$,$8^{th}$ and $11^{th}$ places. The very first time they entered the Isle of Man T.T. race, the Honda team won the Team Prize.

Soichiro was jubilant.

"Even though we could not win the Championship this time," the team captain said, "We can learn a lot from our experience, and we still use this knowledge when we race next time. We did not have very much engine trouble, and we never quit. Those are our strengths!"

Two years later, in 1961, the Honda team swept the first five places of the Isle of Mann T.T. Race.

"An Oriental Miracle!" The international mass media gave Honda high praise indeed. Soichiro had manufactured motorbikes for ten years, and yet he challenged motorbike makers who had been in business for fifty years. It was impossible at first for him to win races, but with racing experience, he upgraded his skills.

"If someone has an idea, tries it out, and successfully invents something, I want to meet that person." Soichiro said. "I believe that when we face a challenge, we want to use our wisdom to overcome the problem by inventing something new and better. Only when humans get into desperate situations, do we have real power. Necessity is the mother of invention. We can accomplish almost anything if we try."

# Chapter 8

## Bathrooms

Soichiro was very picky about bathrooms. "The bathroom revealed the owner's character. Every time I visited a person's house, I tried to use the bathroom. Even though the guest room might be beautiful and clean, if the bathroom was dirty, I never wanted to make that person a friend," Soichiro said.

Soichiro thought his house was important because he lived there every day. He tried to make it as pleasant a place as possible. He did not want to have a summer house or cottage. Instead, he used hotels.

"A hotel is a moving cottage," he said.

He thought having a cottages or summer houses was a waste of money, because one does not live there all the time.

Soichiro thought carefully when he put a restroom into his factory or office building. He placed a clean, bright and beautiful restroom in a place where everyone would walk the same distance to it; that made all employees happy.

Once Soichiro and a *gaijin* (a foreigner) drank sake together. The *gaijin* vomited at midnight. A maid cleaned up the mess and threw it away in the bathroom—an old-fashioned style toilet.

The next morning, the *gaijin* said, "Where is my denture?"

O. Snow—Who Was Honda?

Soichiro thought, *someone should go into the toilet and look for it.* But he knew no one wanted to go into the toilet bowl. *I must do it! I must show people: people must learn to do that which no one wants to do! It will be a good lesson!* So he undressed and went to the bathroom and looked for the denture. He placed his hands into the toilet bowl. Soon he found it. He washed, disinfected, and smelled it. There was no odor, so he washed it again and gave it to the *gaijin.* The *gaijin* was jubilant.

Everyone's eyes popped out.

"I didn't care." Soichiro said with a smile. "Sometimes I did such things."

# Chapter 9

## Automobile Business

Soichiro always motivated his employees by saying," How can I best use the time that is freely given us? This is the secret of success." He also said, "Do not be afraid of failing, but be afraid of not trying."

Even after Honda was successful in exporting motorbikes, Soichiro had another dream. He wanted to make cars. This was his ultimate goal. But his company did not have enough money because he spent so much on the Isle of Mann T.T. Race. He also built a new factory. Researching, manufacturing and selling automobiles are very expensive tasks. So Honda had to sell many motorbikes to earn enough capital to manufacture cars.

Soichiro continued producing motorbikes while he was waiting for the right time to enter the automobile market. He was prepared to take his time, but the Japanese government suggested that he should not expand his company into car manufacturing. The American government had asked the Japanese to simplify trade because imported cars had so many regulations. But if Japan agreed to this, the big three automobile companies—GM, Ford and Chrysler—would rush into Japan.

To survive the competition of foreign cars, the Japanese government official thought it best to merge Japanese automobile companies into one large, strong company. "We don't need any more car companies," one Japanese official said. If this proposal were enacted into law, Honda would not be able to make cars in the future.

"We have to make cars before the law goes into effect," Soichiro demanded. "We must make an extra-small sports car!"

"But a sports car usually needs a large frame," an engineer said.

"We have highly advanced skill in using a small engine that can produce large horsepower," Soichiro replied.

"Oh, I see," the engineer said. "Placing a small motorbike's engine into a small car. This is a new idea!"

Soichiro developed a light sport car and a light track car as soon as possible. And he exhibited all three cars at the Japanese auto show in 1962—making a brilliant debut.

In 1963, Honda sold the light track T-360, S-360 and the sports car S-500 that featured Honda's original engine, different from any other sports cars produced in Europe.

Soichiro also developed a racing engine so that he could realize his dream of changing the Formula One—F 1 Grand Prix, the world's number one racing series. All the other car companies were shocked. Honda had expertise with motorbikes, but he was new to the car world and had much to learn. Still Soichiro had prepared for F 1 racing two years earlier.

In 1964, Honda began to compete in F 1 racing, and in October 1965, the Honda team participated in the Mexican Grand Prize. Many engineering teams could not prepare an engine for the higher altitudes of the Mexican race, but Director Nakamura already had experience from working on fighter planes. He knew how to build an engine to function well in thin air. Honda won the championship. The director sent a telegram to Soichiro, saying: "Came, Saw, Won, Nakamura."

At that time, Soichiro could not make a car that was popular with the public, but he believed "every failure is a stepping stone to success." Then Honda made a lightweight N360, and it was a big hit. Honda had finally received recognition as an automobile maker.

# Ayrton Senna

## (1960—1994)

From 1980 to 1990, Ayrton Senna, a league racer, created an F1 boom of popularity in Japan with his racing skills. Many consider him the greatest racing driver of all time.

He was the most exciting racer: "I very much enjoyed watching him race," Soichiro said.

Senna was born in Brazil in 1960. He debuted as an F 1 auto racer in1984. In 1988 he won his first world championship.

"I will make a more powerful engine for you next year," Soichiro told him. Senna was impressed. After that Senna called Soichiro "My Japanese father."

Senna won three championships with cars using Honda engines.

In 1991, Senna received news of Soichiro's death. Soon after, Senna wore a black mourning band. When he won the Hungary Grand Prix, he said, "I dedicate this victory to Soichiro Honda."

In 1994, Senna died racing in the San Marino Grand Prix.

# Janson Button

## (1980-- )

Janson was born in England and started kart racing when he was only eight. One year later he took first place in the British Super Prix. In 1999 he debuted as an F 3 racer. He did well, and he first raced an F 1 in 2000. He won many races, but he didn't win a championship for six years.

In 2006, in the Hungarian Grand Prix, Janson won his first championship race in a car with Honda engine. He has felt strongly attached to Honda ever since.

# Chapter 10
## Developing the Cleanest Engine

Soichiro wanted to keep entering the F 1 race, but pollution from excess exhaust had become a world problem. He gave up racing and focused on how to reduce car pollution, which was much more important.

In 1970, America passed the Masaki automobile regulation, reducing ninety percent of exhaust pollution.

Soichiro was excited and said, "We have to develop an engine that produces clean exhaust. It will be easy to comply with this law. All automobile makers have the same challenge— starting from zero. This is an excellent chance."

Soon the Honda Company established two teams to satisfy the Masaki regulation. Sixty people were selected to develop a catalyst formula that would reduce exhaust pollution, and seven people were selected to develop an engine that would produce cleaner exhaust.

If Honda could develop cleaner engines that produced fewer toxic emissions, the company could help reduce pollution in the world. But the technology that required was new to Honda engineers, and the work was slow. Soichiro announced, "We are developing a new engine!" He showed an example to the public and promised. "We are going to achieve success."

His engineers felt refreshed and gained new motivation.

They worked hard day after day. For the engine to burn the gas completely, one-part gas mixed with 14.8 parts air combusted well, but not cleanly. Toxic substances were produced and expelled in the exhaust. So they tried mixing in more air, but then the gasoline did not burn as efficiently.

Soichiro thought about engines all the time, even in his dreams. One morning, he looked at the baked eggs that his wife had cooked. They were very beautifully done. Soichiro asked, "How can you cook them so perfectly?"

"If you use low heat and cook them slowly, they will not burn," she answered.

"Slowly and evenly …" Soichiro had an idea.

He took the eggs, went to the office, and said to the staff. "Just like you were baking these eggs, you must burn the gas slowly, and then the gas will burn completely."

"Oh! Slowly," one of them shouted. "If we make a denser mix use for only part of the fire, and supply a thinner mix for the other part, we can burn the gas and air mixture more slowly!"

"We have to make two chambers: one for the thicker mixture and one for the thinner mixture," Soichiro suggested.

"Oyaji-san (Daddy-san), that's it!" (The employees called Soichiro "Oyaji-san.")

"Okay, you take care of the rest. If this method is successful, Honda's cars will be all over the world. I want to be more successful than GM or Ford!"

Then suddenly, the team members put their heads down and became silent.

"What the matter with you?" Soichiro asked.

"Oyaji-san. We are developing this engine not for Honda, but for people who suffer from polluting exhaust emission."

Soichiro was silent and left the room. *Yes, the young people are right. I am getting old. It is time to retire,* he thought.

In December 1972, Honda's CVCC engine passed the Masaki regulation, the first engine to accomplish this. Honda used the new engine for the Honda Civic, a small car but roomy inside and reasonably priced. The Honda Civic was a big success and was exported all over the world, making the company a world leader in automobile production.

For this accomplishment, Soichiro became a member of the Automobile Hall of Fame in 1989. He was the first Japanese selected for his honor.

# Chapter 11
## <u>Finding the Right Timing</u>

"A president should monitor his health and competence, so he will know when it is time to retire and to transfer his position to younger people," Soichiro said.

He loved to repair cars. Even though he was the president of Honda motors, he often crawled under cars and enjoyed fixing them.

"My right and my left hands are different," Soichiro said. "My right hand is bigger and thicker than my left. My left hand has many scars. I always held tools in my right hand. My left was a victim. My nails broke many times, but new nails soon grew out before long. My forefinger and thumb are half inches shorter because I cut them with blades while repairing. A drill poked through into my hand. I am strong despite my injuries. My old scars are my treasures, and they remind me of the past fifty years."

But when cars became more and more computerized, he didn't know how to fix them. As he aged, he could not keep up with the advancements of technology. He felt it was time to retire and make room for young people who would also grow stronger. Soichiro always said, "Young people are making advanced technology. Youth is power!"

In October 1973, Soichiro and vice president Fujisawa both retired. "I don't want to get in the way of young people!" Soichiro said.

O. Snow—Who Was Honda?

Soichiro chose forty-five-year-old Kiyoshi Kawashima to be the second president: "You can run the business any way you like, but don't let people form a negative opinion of Honda," Soichiro warned.

When Soichiro retired, he had a hard time leaving the work he loved. When morning came, he wanted to go to work; but if he went there, he would not really be retired. And he did not want his prestige to interfere with the young people who were now running the business. So he tried not to go back to the office or the factory.

"Landing is important," Soichiro always said. "If a man can't make a good landing—the final stage—his life has not been successful." His retirement came at just the right time for him, and his successful "Landing" amazed people.

O. Snow—Who Was Honda?

Soichiro also refused to make speeches about his business success. Instead, he was busy visiting all his employees with his wife Sachi, shaking hands with each employee and thanking them for their service to his company. Meeting all his workers took two years—1974 to 1976.

After that, Soichiro undertook the art of Japanese painting. He began by drawing sketches. As he was a technician, it was very important to him that the picture's size must be exactly to scale. If he wanted to draw half sizes, he drew exactly one-half. If not, his heart ached. He was a perfectionist.

In 1980, he had an opportunity to visit Marc Chagall (1887-1985), a famous artist who lived in southern France. Soichiro was seventy-four and Chagall was ninety-three. They met at

Chagall's house. They enjoyed meeting each other very much, and after one hour, Soichiro gave a Japanese painting set to Chagall. Chagall was very pleased and asked Soichiro how to use it. Soon after, Chagall took the tools and went to his studio without saying goodbye.

Later Soichiro said, "As soon as possible, Chagall wanted to paint with his new tools. I very much envied his passion and curiosity."

Soichiro was active into his eighties, but eventually his liver failed and he was hospitalized. He asked his wife, "Sachi-san, would you support me and help me walk a little?" Sachi guided him slowly in the hospital bedroom and told him when to move his feet. "Right, left, right, left …" and they walked as if it were their final dance together.

## O. Snow—Who Was Honda?

He said, "I don't want to have a company-sponsored funeral because it might cause a traffic jam. Instead, do something to say 'thank you' to the public."

He cared about people to the last minutes of his life.

On August 5, 1991, Soichiro died at the age of eighty-four.

At his request, the funeral service was held with only his family members in attendance. That night, there was noise outside. The next morning, when Sachi went outside, her eyes opened wide in surprise to see a lot of flowers shining in the morning sun. During the night, many young people who loved motorbikes, F 1 racing and the fastest cars in the world had left those flowers as their farewell.

O. Snow—Who Was Honda?

The Honda corporation had a "Thank You" farewell celebration. Sixty-two thousand people mourned for Soichiro Honda.

Soichiro was loved by young and old alike.

# Chapter 12

## Heart

Soichiro established two companies for handicapped people. In 1978 Soichiro and Masaru Ibuka, the president of the SONY Corporation, visited a handicapped facility. "Taiyo no Ie" (House of Sun). Soichiro saw that handicapped people worked seriously. *I want to help them, too!* he thought.

In 1981 Soichiro established "Honda Taiyo" (Sun of Honda) and "Kibo no Sato Honda" (Honda Home of Hope) in 1992.

After Soichiro died, the Honda Corporation established a third facility, "Honda R & D Taiyo" (R & D Sun of Honda).

O. Snow—Who Was Honda?

Many handicapped people work enthusiastically at these three companies and are grateful for the opportunity to earn an income and enjoy the independence it brings them.

Before and after Soichiro retired, he poured his heart out to repay society for his success. In 1960 he built a playground.

After Soichiro died, the Honda team established four categories of community contributions:

"Improving activity for children."

"Protecting the environment."

"Maintaining traffic safety."

"Providing regional activity."

Honda's work with children was established in 2002 and featured a "children's idea contest." The program encouraged young people to dream about their future and work toward the fulfillment of their dreams, just as Soichiro had done.

In 2006 Honda established a beach cleaning initiative called "walking with bare feet on the beach." Soichiro's heart for invention, facing new challenges and the betterment of society lives on in the Honda Company as he wished.

# Masasru Ibuka

## (1908-1997)

Masaru Ibuka, who established the Sony Corporation, was born in Nikko, Tochigi. After he graduated from Waseda University, he established Tokyo Tsusin Kogyo (now called Sony), with his business partner, Akira Morishita. They made tape recorders, transistor radios and "walkmans" … With these and other products, they developed Sony into a worldwide corporation.

Masaru and Soichiro became friends soon after Masaru started his company. Soichiro was cheerful with a lively personality, while Masaru was a very calm and quiet person. But they were both engineers and passionate about making "something new." They had much in common. Moreover, they loved to contribute to society, and they didn't refuse if someone asked them to do just that.

Soichiro was two years senior to Masaru. Masaru called Soichiro "big brother." After Soichiro died, Masaru published *My Friend Soichiro Honda* to share Soichiro's great personality.

# Chapter 13

## The Power of Dream

Soichiro loved the word "dream" and worked hard to achieve it. "The Power of Dream" was his catch phrase, and the Honda Corporation adopted these words as the company motto in 2006.

Soichiro also wanted to develop an airplane, but that dream did not come true in his lifetime. However, in 1986 the Honda team of engineers developed a small plane. After further progress, in 2003, they completed the Honda jet. It was very expensive, but the Honda jet makers received orders from both America and Europe.

O. Snow—Who Was Honda?

In 1986, Honda developed a robot but did not officially announce it until 1996. The P-2 robot had two legs and amazed the world with its smooth movement. Then, in 2002, another robot named ASIMO was revealed to the public and became popular. By 2005, the robot could dance and walk up and down stairs at the speed of 3.7 MPH.

The Honda team still seeks to carry out Soichiro's creative dream.

# Chapter 14
## Memories of Soichiro Honda

## **Time Is Life**

Soichiro's father was very strict about using time well. He said, "Money or health is not given equally, but God has given everyone a crucial amount of time. How to use this precious time is the secret of success."

Soichiro agreed. He was never late to meetings. He tried not to waste time because he realized how valuable it was.

# Do Not Be Afraid of Failing, But Be Afraid of Trying Nothing

Soichiro kept challenging all his life. He failed 99 percent of the time, but his one percent success gave him his creative victory.

"People have a right to fail, but this right will lead to success. You must do the things you really like," Soichiro said. "Then you can overcome problems. If you do things you don't like, you won't be able to solve your problems."

## Making 120 % of products

If he seeks to be 100 percent accurate, he might aim at one percent of error. In order not to make any mistakes, Soichiro sought to be 120 percent accurate.

## Brain Exercise

Japan is only the size of California. There is no gold, silver or oil.

"There are no resources but the people," Soichiro said. "Humans are the most valuable resource, but everyone must offer ideas and hard work to survive in Japan."

The Honda Corporation has an "idea contest." If the idea is excellent, they pay for it and use it.

## Children Without Mischief
## Have No Charm

Though Soichiro was a mischievous child, his mischief    showed that he had the creativity to make something new. When a child is mischievous, he is full of originality and ingenuity. The child must enjoy his ideas.

"When I remember such mischief, I am nostalgic," Soichiro admitted later. "Mischief is unavoidable in children. They are trying to express something through their antics. Mischievous children have a great future. If a child always follows what his parents say, it seems strange.

"In mischief there is the bud of a creative personality. If a child studies all the time just to make good grades, looks at people's faces to judge their moods, and tries to be a good boy, he cannot work creatively or eagerly at his job. A person who takes the long view and has a strong faith in his own beliefs is the kind of person who will do dynamic work."

## I Would Not Try
## If It Were Not For the People

Soichiro was dynamic but also sensitive. As a president, he always said these words: "I wanted to make good products, which meant I wanted to make people happy."

## <u>I Want to Make</u>
## <u>a Unique Company</u>

Soichiro insisted on egalitarianism and the merit system. He tried to make an environment where subordinates could exchange ideas with their superiors. Honda's office is not private. Except for the president, all officials sit in one room so they can talk freely and determine policy. And if someone has a good idea, he can talk to everyone at once. This style is known as Honda's freely run corporate culture.

# Take it Back!

Soichiro did not like to receive any gifts from his employees. If someone brought him a bottle of whisky, he would say: "I don't want to receive it. Please take it back!"

Many Japanese companies give something to their superiors twice a year. But Honda's employees do not have to do that. "Are they working for the company or for their supervisor?" Soichiro asked. He did not want his employees to confuse their loyalties. "It is so stupid that a person who has much money should receive gifts and a person who doesn't have money should give gifts. If someone gives a gift, it should be the president to the employees. That is reasonable," Soichiro said.

In September 1963, Soichiro celebrated the 15th anniversary of his foundation. He invited his 8,000 employees to stay one night in Kyoto—it cost a hundred million yen ($1,000,000 U.S.D.) for the dinner party and made big news in the public media.

## **Praising is Difficult**

Soichiro rarely praised people. If he praised someone, someone else might think "I did that, too. Why didn't he praise me?" Such a person is jealous.

"Many people have a high opinion of themselves. Be careful when you praise someone,"

Soichiro said. "I always consider that someone else may be jealous. Jealousy is a strong feeling. Praising is difficult."

## A Good Landing Is Important

"A president must recognize his own limitations. When I feel old, I must give my position to someone young. After I am retired, I do not want to bother them," Soichiro said. "If you can't manage a good landing, your life has not been successful."

## **He Was a Gifted Person**

Soichiro had an expert knowledge of electronics, machinery and chemistry. Many people were shocked when they found out that he had only graduated from elementary school.

Soichiro always told his new employees, "If you depend on what you already know, you can't create new knowledge." He always thought that real knowledge is gained by having experience in the field and then using one's brain power.

Soichiro often said, "Through your basic knowledge and creativity, solve each problem. Honda doesn't care about your educational background."

## Oyaji-san Spoke from His Heart

Employees called Soichiro "Oyaji-san" (Daddy-san). When Soichiro was happy, he hugged his employees. Soichiro's enthusiastic spoken manner charmed many people.

## Time Line of Soichiro Honda's Life

1906—Soichiro was born in Shizuoka, Japan.

1922—After he graduated from Koto elementary school, he worked at Art Shokai in Tokyo, an automobile repair factory.

1923—The Great Kanto Earthquake.

1928—Established Hamamatsu Art Shokai.

1931—Invented the iron spoke (long thin bar on tire). Called "Edison" in Hamamatsu.

O. Snow—Who Was Honda?

1933—Married to Sachi Isobe, a school teacher

1937—Established Tokaiseiki Jukogyo Co. and produced piston rings.

1948—Established Honda Giken Kogyo Co., which made many motorcycles.

1959—First time entered the Isle of Man T.T. Race.

1961—Honda swept the first five places at the Isle of Man T.T. race.

1962—Made automobiles.

1964—Challenged to F1 GP

1965--Won the championship at F 1 Mexico GP.

1972—Developed low-pollution Honda CVCC engine and passed first in the world for American exhaust gas regulation, Masaki law regularity.

1973—Retired as president.

1974-1976—Visited all of his employees to say "thank you," and shook hands.

1980—After he retired, he was interested in Japanese painting and visited Marc Chagall in France.

1989—Became the first Japanese member of AHF (Automobile Hall of Fame).

1991—Soichiro Honda died at the age of 84.

# The Time Line of the World

1908—Ford Company made Type T Ford Automobile.

1913—Ford Company produced many cars.

1914—World War I broke out.

1939—World War II began.

1945—Atomic bomb dropped on Hiroshima.

1949—Hideki Yukawa received Noble Prize for physics.

1951—AU.S.—Japan Security Treaty was enacted.

1963—President Kennedy assassinated.

1964—Tokyo Olympics opened.

1969—Neil Armstrong became the first person to walk on the moon.

1970—In America, established Masaki law regulation.

1972—Sapporo Winter Olympics opened.

1981—Prince Charles married Lady Diana Spencer.

1989—Berlin Wall falls.

# References

Honda, Soichiro. *Eteni Ho Agete.* (Be on Song). Kokubunsha (2014)

Honda, Soichiro. *Konohitowo Miyo! (The Man Who Made World History!)* Popura Sha. (2013)

Honda, Soichiro. *Yaritaikoto wo Yare. (You Must Do What You Like.)* Gakugei Shupanbu (2014)

Nakahata, Satoru. Honda Soichiro—Sekaiichi Hayai Kurumawo Tsukutta Otoko. (Soichiro Honda—the Man Who Made the Fastest Car in the World.) Shogkukan (1996-2014)

# Acknowledgements

I want to give a special word of thanks to many of my friends.

Thank you to Mr. Ed Bacon, who taught me until two weeks before he died.

Thank you to Ms. Kathryn Brownlow, my counselor, a beautiful, humble and intelligent writer.

Thank you to my high school mate, Yoko Todome, who encouraged me to write this book.

Thank you to Dr. William Ruehlmann and Dr. David G. Clark, who read the entire manuscript and gave me excellent advice.

Thank you to Jay Antol, who made this cover and his encouragement.

Thank you for Tara Moeller and Mo Moeller's special help.

Thank you to Virginia Beach Writers, Hampton Roads Writers, Great Neck Book club and Virginia Beach Public Library.

May God bless all.

# O. Snow

Born in a snow town in Japan, she reads, writes and speaks both English and Japanese.

She won third place at the Christopher Newport University non-fiction competition in 2017, first place at the Christopher Newport University fiction competition in 2016 and honorable mention at the Hampton Roads Writers non-fiction competition in 2015. She has published in the *Virginian-Pilot* newspaper, *RDH* (Registered Dental hygienist) magazine and *ProQuest.* She continues to write every day.

She likes to laugh, to cry, to learn something new and to be touched when she reads. She enjoys taking care of her vegetable garden, walking, knitting and making quilts.

She was a volunteer at the Virginia Beach Public Library for more than twenty years.

## Also by O. Snow

*A Dog Lover* (Young Adult fiction.)
*Short Stories.*